KITE

Wales

ove

s Tale (RSPB 1991) by the same author

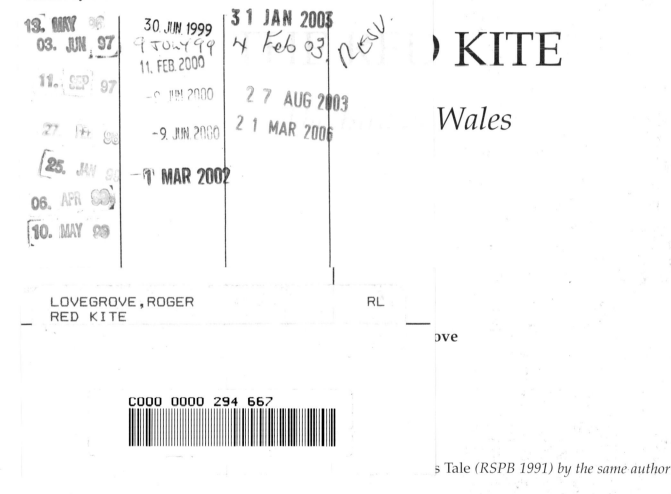

© The Royal Society for the Protection of Birds 1995

ISBN 1 85902 252 9

Photographic credits:
front cover – *Manfred Danegger (NHPA)*
frontispiece – *Watercolour of red kite in oak tree by Colin Woolf*
page 7 FLPA; page 12,13 Manfred Danegger (NHPA); page 16,26,27 C H Gomersall (RSPB); page 30,31 Jase Luis Gonzales Grande (Bruce Coleman Ltd); page 32 R J C Blewitt; page 32 RSPB; page 33 Oxford Scientific Films; page 34,35 RSPB; page 36 Liz and Tony Bomford (Ardea); page 37 RSPB; page 38 Manfred Danegger (NHPA); page 39 Jose Luis Ganzales Grande (Bruce Coleman Ltd); page 40,41 FLPA; page 42,43 C H Gomersall (RSPB); page 44,45 Liz and Tony Bomford (Ardea); page 45 C H Gomersall (RSPB); page 46 Jose Luis Gonzales Grande (Bruce Coleman Ltd).

Line Drawings: *Darren Rees*

Map: *Drawing Attention*

Publishers: *Gomer Press/Kite Country*

Printed: *Gomer Press, Llandysul, Dyfed.*

Contents

1 Seeing Red Kites in Wales

Because the red kite is such a spectacular bird, it is understandably the ambition of many people, birdwatchers and general public alike, to see it in the wild. It is at the very top of the list of those species in Britain which people are most keen to see. However, because it has also been so rare during the 20th century and is so vulnerable to disturbance during the breeding season (the time of year, of course, when most people visit the countryside), it has been essential to discourage people from coming to Wales to look for it. Now, however, the cloak of secrecy can at last be very carefully and cautiously lifted. Thanks to various conservation measures the kite's population in Wales has gradually strengthened in recent years and has grown steadily past 100 pairs. Now the advantage lies in providing facilities where people can learn more about this remarkable bird and have a better opportunity of seeing it. With the kite's population at this enhanced level and its future on a slightly better footing, there is a clear benefit in assisting visitors to see birds in circumstances where they will not endanger them, rather than risk people searching the countryside themselves.

Thus it was, in 1994, that the Kite Country Project was launched as a green tourism initiative, led by the RSPB and comprising five local authorities in the project area, together with the Development Board for Rural Wales, Wales Tourist Board and the Countryside Council for Wales. The project, funded by the Welsh

Office for its initial years, is developing information centres and outdoor facilities throughout central Wales to provide increased information for visitors on a wide spectrum of wildlife, particularly birds of prey. These facilities include winter feeding stations, live pictures from nest sites of kites and several other birds of prey beamed into centres, displays, interactive exhibitions and printed literature. In addition, there is an emphasis on enabling people to see kites and other species in their natural surroundings without causing disturbance to the birds themselves.

By far the best and easiest time of year to see red kites is in winter. At this season the birds are more visible against the bare landscape, making the most of the brief daylight hours. Furthermore they tend to roost communally in favoured locations and can be lured easily to places where food is regularly provided for them. The Kite County Project has developed one major winter feeding site on Gigrin Farm, Rhayader, where outstanding views of large numbers of kites can be almost guaranteed (except in the very worst of weather!) daily between November and the end of February. Subsidiary feeding stations may be developed from time to time at other locations; at Tregaron a long–established feeding site also exists which is independent of the Kite Country Project. Remember, red kites are still rare and vulnerable birds. Great damage can be done by disturbing them during the nesting season. Up-to-date information on how best to see the birds at a particular time of year can be obtained from the RSPB Wales Office (telephone 01686 624143). Always observe the following code:

• Look for red kites by scanning the sky and the skyline. Never attempt to find kite nests – or the nests of other species!

• When in the countryside keep to rights of way and observe the country code. Do not go onto private land; farmers and landowners are the kite's best friends but are seriously irritated by trespass.

• If you believe you are near nesting kites, move away immediately. Ever–present carrion crows are very quick to prey on eggs that are left unguarded if the kites are disturbed.

• Remember, it is an offence, punishable by fines up to £5,000 knowingly to disturb kites at the nest site.

2 The Red Kite

The red kite is unarguably a Welsh bird but, more than that, it is by common accord the bird of Wales. It also happens to be both extremely rare and extremely beautiful: arguably the most beautiful bird of prey in Britain. For that matter there is no other bird of prey throughout the whole of the kite's range in Europe to rival its aerial grace or the fiery beauty of its plumage. For us in Britain there is the additional thrill that it is such a very rare bird – that it has, quite literally, been clawed back against all the odds from the very edge of extinction.

The red kite is one of our larger birds of prey, with a body length of over 60 cm and long narrow wings with a span well in excess of 170 cm. Its name reflects the rusty chestnut-red of its body and upper tail. The kite's head is pale greyish-white. As it wheels in the sunlight, the tawny upperparts are accentuated by a broad crescent of white, curving across the inner part of the wings. From below, the long forked tail is pale grey with narrow bands on the inner web giving a barred effect, but the pattern of the kite's underwing is most striking: the colour is a lustrous chestnut–brown,

extending along the leading edge of the wings to the carpal joints; behind them the secondaries are banded grey with several darker bars producing a dark trailing edge. It is the primary feathers which produce the startling contrast of colour. The long, fingered primaries are strongly tipped with black but their bases are extensively white to produce a vividly contrasting patch on the underwing, visible at a considerable distance. The kite's legs and feet are bright lemon-yellow – often detectable in flight – and the hooded eye, ringed with lemon, is the colour of burnished amber.

However, no picture in words can adequately convey the true beauty and grace of the red kite. It is only in flight that the bird's incomparable grace is seen and a full appreciation of its colours becomes possible. It is in every way a bird of the air, designed and equipped to fly with buoyant grace and economy of effort. Much of its time is spent in soaring, often in long periods high above the valleys in which it lives. As it rises, it manoeuvres to maximise the benefit from each breath of wind and every lift of

thermal. It will circle round and round, gradually gaining height and all the time balancing, steering and adjusting by the ceaseless twisting and fanning of its long flexuous tail. No bird uses its tail more in flight than does the kite; no bird is more ethereal on the wing, drifting and floating with gossamer lightness. Because it is so disproportionately light for its size, the red kite floats and drifts with a lazy ease and buoyancy which no other bird, not even a harrier, can match. It can check and hold on the wing or pivot and pirouette with the delicacy and precision of a ballerina. As it swings round, the light will suddenly catch its plumage and fire the russet red of the body and the upper tail or highlight the translucent patches on the underwing and the white crescents above; at

such a moment one never fails to catch one's breath.

The two sexes are virtually identical. Only those who are really familiar with the birds can claim to separate males from females with certainty. The female's wings tend to be proportionately longer and broader than the male's; the kite is an amazingly agile bird on the wing but the male tends to be even more buoyant in flight and is distinctly more agile. He uses his wings much more freely and independently of each other than the female does; her wingbeats are usually more constant, deep and rhythmical. Male birds also use their tails constantly, fanning, twisting and flexing the whole while.

. . . .

Previous page: In the early mornings on damp or dewy days, kites often spend time walking on short grassland picking up earthworms and beetles.

3 Kite Country

In Wales the red kite is still a bird of the thinly populated hill country. Its home is the hanging oakwoods of the steep–sided valleys of central Wales. In these woods and valleys it finds the quietness and security it needs for resting during the daytime and roosting at night. During spring and summer the oakwoods become the focus for breeding and although in Wales nests are often sited in fairly large or continuous areas of woodland, some nests are built in small copses, narrow strips of shelter-belt in the hills or even scattered hedgerow trees. In these respects the kite is indeed a woodland bird but, at the same time, it is more accurate to see these woodlands as the focal point of the kite's daily life, within which it has its base but from which it ranges for considerable distances and for long periods on feeding expeditions. Thus, as well as being a woodland bird, it is equally a bird of open country, requiring extensive areas with low vegetation over which to hunt. It finds its food not in woodland but in a wide range of open habitats, from moorland and mountain sheepwalk to enclosed fields of the valley bottom, bracken hillsides, watersides and even rural refuse sites.

Kite Country epitomises the essence of rural Wales: an intimate mixture of small fields, wooded hedgerows and copses with open sheep-walk on the hilltops. This countryside is the heartland of the red kite in Wales, for it is here in the quietness of remote valleys and woodlands that the precious remnant population of kites has clung on in the fastness of a countryside which is itself steeped in mystery and secrecy; here a different language is spoken, visitors may sometimes be conscious of a feeling of intrusion when they wander the remoter lanes and hillsides in the kite's domain. Here on wild hills and in valleys of crags, tumbling streams and ancient woodlands it is as if an unseen eye is watching and the kite is wrapped in a protective cloak of Celtic mystique: on the one hand fugitive from man over the years but on the other hand fiercely protected by him in remote farmsteads and lonely communities. In the kite's valleys and hillsides the lingering spirits of the past are easily imagined and the kite represents in many ways the ineffable, indefinable spirit of a Celtic culture, pushed like the kite itself to the western fringes of our island, defensive of its world and jealous of its uniqueness.

The woodlands which represent the kite's retreat are themselves evocative and characteristic of western areas where rainfall is high and growing conditions are often harsh. Here, the oaks do not grow tall and mighty as they do in softer climates where the lowland pedunculate oak prospers; these are durmast (or sessile) oaks, clinging low and firm-footed to the hill sides, their roots locked into myriad fissures between and around moss-covered boulders. Often they are festooned with mosses, lichens and epiphytic ferns. They support a limitless supply of food for song birds through the year and are the summer home of other special Welsh birds such as wood warbler, tree pipit, redstart and pied flycatcher.

. . . .

4 Lifestyle

Welsh red kites are resident. They remain in the general area of their breeding range throughout the year and are not migratory as many of the continental birds necessarily are; they leave as winter sets in and move to warmer areas in southern France and Iberia. Although the Welsh breeding population is sedentary, some of the young birds wander off in their first autumn, and recoveries of ringed birds confirm that such wanderers may travel considerable distances in a wide variety of directions, although most seem to head south–eastwards. Some certainly continue their wanderings through their first year or even longer, before they make their way back to their natal areas and prepare to join the breeding population.

Most of the breeding birds are faithful to their partners throughout their reproductive life and experienced pairs invariably have an increased likelihood of breeding successfully. Thus they normally pair for life although the bond may be looser in winter than during the breeding season as individuals wander more widely in search of good feeding sources. During

~ THE RED KITE ~

~   THE RED KITE   ~

fine weather as early as January or February pairs will meet near their nesting sites where they may take part in high circling displays often rising to great heights and not infrequently joining with neighbouring pairs. These somewhat unspectacular flights are about as near as the kites come to genuine display even as the season intensifies in March and April. Occasionally mutual displays may be more exciting and demonstrable, with a pair grasping talons and cartwheeling giddily towards the ground before separating and rising again. It is usually only at this time of year that one may hear the high-pitched whistling call of the male, thinner and more shrill than the melancholy mewing of the buzzard.

Nesting takes place in late March and April and the nest is an untidy affair of sticks which are collected from the ground or occasionally broken from trees or bushes. Building is carried out by both birds and is at its most intense in the relatively short period in the very early hours of daylight. In Wales the nest is

Previous page: Carrion crows and other corvids are a constant threat to nests during the breeding season, but in return, kites prey on nesting corvids to feed their young.

invariably lined with sheep's wool; scraps of rubbish, cloth, plastic, coloured string, may be collected to decorate the nest but never greenery in the manner of a buzzard's nest. The nest is usually in the main fork of a large tree or in the fork of upper branches maybe as high as 20 m above the ground. Hanging oakwoods are favoured but beech, birch, alder or several species of conifer are sometimes used.

Eggs are usually laid in early April and most clutches are complete by the middle of that month. The majority (about 75%) of clutches in Wales consist of two eggs while a slightly increasing percentage (about 20%) of pairs produces three eggs. Very occasionally as many as four eggs may be produced. Nests with single eggs are usually attributable to young females laying for the first time at an age of perhaps two or three years. Incubation lasts 31 or 32 days but because the eggs are laid at about three–day intervals the overall hatching period may last as long as 37 to 38 days from the laying of the first egg to the emergence of the last chick. The majority of the incubation is carried out by the female, which has only short spells off the nest each day when she is relieved by the male. This means that she is fed at the nest by her partner most of the time and leaves the nest to feed for herself, usually in the early morning. Once the chicks hatch they are carefully brooded by the female for the first two weeks or more while the male does most of the hunting. The fledging period lasts between seven and nine weeks depending partly on the availability of food and the number of chicks to be fed.

The red kite is a bird of prey and a fairly catholic feeder although it is first and foremost a scavenger and opportunist. In Wales it profits particularly from the sheep carrion resulting from the hill farming but also from human waste too: it is a regular visitor to refuse tips. At the same time it is also a true predator taking a wide variety of live prey at certain seasons, ranging from earthworms (which it often collects by walking the ground in the damp fields of early morning) to small mammals, amphibians and birds – particularly nestlings of magpies and crows – in May and June at which time it also takes young rabbits to feed to nestlings. Despite being a relatively large bird it is neither a particularly strong nor aggressive one. Although it eats much sheep carrion it is not capable of opening up sheep or lamb carcases by itself and has to wait until more powerful birds such as a ravens or buzzards have made the first inroads before it will

attempt to feed. Even then, the kite is often subordinate to others at the carcase and will achieve most of its scraps by robbing carrion crows and other corvids as they fly off from the feast with their pickings.

It does much of its hunting at low level, gliding over the fields and hillsides or towering on deep purposeful wingbeats. As well as this languid flight, elegant soaring and purposeful gliding, the kite is also uniquely agile for a large bird of prey. Its agility on the wing belies its size and it is difficult to appreciate that so large a bird can be so fast on the wing when necessary. As a scavenger the kite is a supreme opportunist; it is not particularly shy and can frequently be seen close to farmsteads or villages. Occasionally it is known to take fish, either dead or alive, from water surfaces.

Outside the breeding season many of the kites roost communally in favoured valleys and at such times it is possible to see congregations of 20 or more birds coming into the roosting area during the short winter afternoons. The birds gather loosely in the area and sit silently in trees before finally moving to selected roost trees in the last glimmerings of light. In winter they wander extensively over central Wales spending more of their time on the lower ground if the weather is inclement or severe.

5 History of the Red Kite in Wales

The history of the red kite in Wales goes back a very long way. In fact the earliest proof of its existence anywhere in Britain comes from bone remnants found in Bacon Hole Cave on the Gower peninsula in south Wales, which was evidently the lair of hyena and other predators and where the finds can be dated to the last inter-glacial period around 120,000 years ago. At the time when Neolithic man arrived in Britain (around 2500 BC) woodland covered most of the land surface and the land would have been unsuited to supporting a large population of a bird such as the red kite, which requires open country over which to hunt. As Neolithic man started the process of woodland clearance and operated a system of slash-and-burn agriculture, a patchwork of clearings developed which was further accelerated in the Bronze Age and, over the centuries, produced a mosaic of open ground and forest which was much more conducive to the needs of a species such as the kite. By the 12th and 13th centuries the kite was certainly an abundant bird of prey throughout much of Britain with a reputation as a thief and a greedy eater. Its status in Wales at that time is even more dimly known than it is for England but there is no reason to suppose that, where the pattern of countryside encouraged it, the red kite was not a very common bird. It is by the Middle Ages that we begin

When feeding is easy in spring and summer, the adults feed early and spend much of the day sitting out of sight in the trees.

to get the real insight into the status of the kite in Britain even though much of the picture still has to be inferred. One conclusion is inescapable and that is that the kite was an extremely numerous species in medieval Britain and almost certainly the most conspicuous and familiar bird of prey. Moreover, it was certainly not restricted to being a rural bird but prospered enormously on the insanitary conditions that characterised many urban areas, especially London where the unpaved and unclean streets and foul watercourses – breeding grounds for such plagues as the Black Death in 1348 – provided abundant feeding for both kites and ravens. By 1465, it was a capital offence to kill a kite or a raven in London, so valued were they as street cleaners and so tame did both become. Indeed the kite was so emboldened and unafraid that it would dare 'to steal food from children, fish from women and 'kerchiefs out of men's hands'. Medieval Britain represented the zenith of the red kite's fortunes. Common in both town and country, it was a feature of daily life for many people throughout the greater part of England, Scotland and Wales. It was during the 16th century that the kite's fortunes were abruptly reversed.

A series of Vermin Acts was introduced in the 16th century which required a long list of 'vermin' species, including red kites, to be killed throughout all the parishes of England and Wales as they represented an alleged threat to the expanding agriculture of the time.

Implementation and interpretation of these Acts was by no means uniform across the parishes of the country and doubtless reflected both the whims and preferences as well as efforts of local parishes and their churchwardens. In Wales very little is known about the pressures that were applied on kites through the enforcement of the Tudor Vermin Acts. In England – and there is no reason for supposing that it was notably different in Wales – the slaughter was often on a huge scale: in one Cheshire parish 411 kites were killed in only 12 years, among an enormous catalogue of other slaughtered wildlife, and in a Kent parish, 380 were killed in one 10-year period. Through the 17th and 18th centuries persecution continued and at the end of the 18th century yet another devastating blow was to occur in the employment of an increasing army of gamekeepers following on from the development of game preservation on country estates after the initiation of the parliamentary enclosures. The combined result of this new tidal wave of persecution was that by 1879 at the latest, kites had bred for the last time in England. In Scotland the story was similar and extermination was complete by the same decade. Thus, only in Wales was there a handful of kites left but even here the picture was very little different from that in other parts of Britain. The kite's former numbers and distribution are very poorly documented in Wales. It was certainly common enough in the southern counties up to the middle of the 19th century but there are only seven written records thereafter in Glamorgan between 1848 and the end of the century. Eggs were taken from a nest near Cardiff as late as 1853 but by the middle of the century it seems that most of Wales had lost its kites although there is some evidence that odd pairs may have survived in the south in Gwent until about 1870.

It was only in the remotest valleys of mid–Wales, in areas sparsely populated and free from gamekeepers that the last handful of red kites survived. The story of their survival and the protection that ensured it is one of the classic stories of bird conservation.

6 Kite Protection

The history of the protection of the red kite in Wales is one which is without parallel throughout the world. Nowhere has there been such an uninterrupted and concerted effort to maintain a fragile breeding population of a species as there has for the kite in the rural fastness of central Wales. Extending over more than 100 years, it is a story of unremitting commitment by successive generations of landowners, rural communities, dedicated individuals and organisations, which has entered the annals of bird protection. In the end it has been a story of success but along the way it has been one of decades of frustration, despair and often apparent failure. It has also been punctuated by acts of betrayal, deceit and duplicity.

By the year 1889 – only a decade or so after the extermination of kites in England and Scotland – there was no more than a tiny handful of pairs of kites known to be left in Wales, centred on the Brecon area. In that year, Cambridge Phillips, the early chronicler of birds in that county, recorded with horror that even then nine or 10 kites had been killed by keepers. He made determined attempts in the years that followed, in conjunction with landowners, to set up a scheme to protect the few remaining pairs through the payment of bounties for successful nests and through sets of 'Instructions to Keepers'. However, it was all to no avail. The killing continued and although a few individuals miraculously survived for a few more years, by 1909 all the birds in the Brecon area had gone.

In 1893, another naturalist, the botanist Professor J H Salter from Aberystwyth University, had stumbled on nesting pairs in the upper Tywi valley, in the area near the modern Llyn Brianne. It is clear that at least two pairs were breeding, possibly more, and although this was their first discovery, it has to be presumed that they had 'always' been present, unknown to people outside the lonely and remote valley. With the demise of the Brecon birds, the Tywi valley became the single eventual focus of the efforts to save the kite and thereby the location for a remarkable story of protection and conservation. Many years later (1968) the RSPB acquired a large landholding in the valley – now the Gwenffrwd and Dinas reserve – to help consolidate the protection efforts that had gone on for so many years before.

In 1903 Salter, incensed by the continuing depredations by egg collectors and taxidermists, wrote a famous letter to the British Ornithologists' Club beseeching the Club to help to save the few remaining pairs. Within days a Kite Preservation Fund had been set up and – at a time when egg collecting was a recognised legal activity – a motion of censure was passed on any member involved in robbery of kite's nests. It was shortly after this, possibly as early as 1905, that the RSPB itself first became involved, probably by subscribing money to the Kite Preservation Fund. That commitment has continued from that day to this – a period of 90 years. Despite the renewed efforts to save the last few pairs, the plundering of nests by egg collectors continued and for the next 40 years the fate of the species hung perilously in the balance. In 1901 there had been four known nests: 30 heartbreaking years followed with minor ups and downs but no marked improvement.

If the zenith for the red kite in Britain was the early Middle Ages, before the introduction of the Tudor Vermin Acts, its nadir was almost certainly the turn of the century or the 1930s when numbers probably fell below 20 individuals; 1940 still produced exactly the same number of nests as 1901, yielding only two fledging young. It was not until 1946 that the total climbed again to seven pairs. Across the years of toil, one of the legendary individuals at the heart of kite

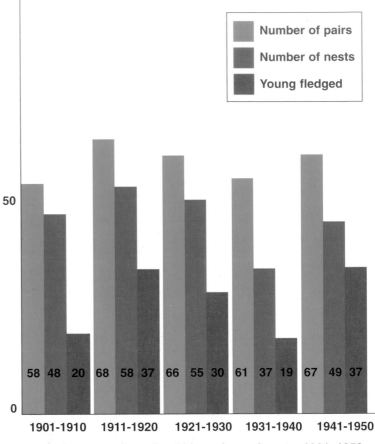

Approximate number of red kite pairs and nests, 1901–1950

protection was the Rev. Edmundes Owen, rector of Llanelwedd, near Builth Wells. As the kite teetered on the brink of extinction, he played a huge and influential role in preventing the final extermination, up to the time of his death in 1934.

The period of the Second World War may have been a time of frustratingly poor information on kites but at

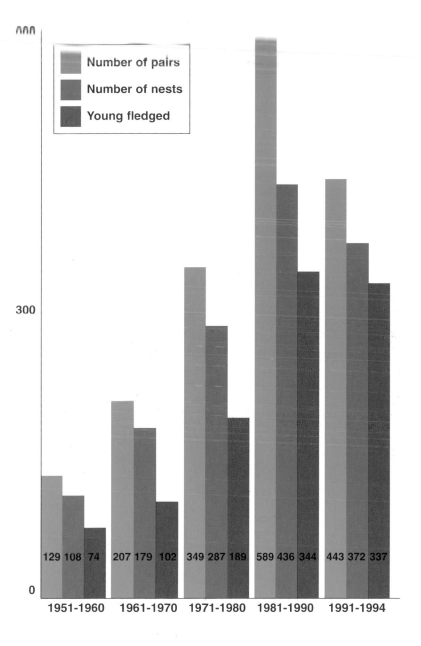

Minimum numbers of red kite pairs and nests, 1951–1994

	1951-1960	1961-1970	1971-1980	1981-1990	1991-1994
Number of pairs	129	207	349	589	443
Number of nests	108	179	287	436	372
Young fledged	74	102	189	344	337

the same time there is no doubt that it marked a modern milestone. As transport was difficult and the younger generation of country people was away in the War, there was less activity, both legal and illegal, involving nests. Fewer pairs were located and recorded but fewer too were robbed. It was at this time that a small but critical corner was turned in the fortunes of the red kite.

In 1964 the Nature Conservancy (now the Countryside Council for Wales) established an office in Aberystwyth and this marked the commencement of a direct input from the statutory conservation body, particularly into important fields of conservation, monitoring and research on red kites.

During the 1950s and 1960s, under the leadership of the redoubtable Captain Vaughan of Rhandirmwyn, the Kite Committee enjoyed the smoothest and best organised period of monitoring and protection that there had yet been. While the 1960s and 1970s were still plagued by egg collectors, the situation very slowly improved although it was not until the late 1980s that the number of known nests in any one year at last passed 50. Since then the annual rise in numbers has been more encouraging and although those who have continued to put so much work into kite protection in latter years deserve nothing but praise, credit must be given to the dedicated individuals of earlier years for holding back the red kite from extinction.

Just how close to the edge of extinction did the kite fall? We now know the answer to this long–standing enigma because through the use of modern techniques of genetic fingerprinting, it has been established by scientists at Nottingham University, working on small blood samples taken from nestling kites over a long period of years, that the entire Welsh population up to 1977 emanated from only one female. In other words, that a single bird, was responsible for producing the offspring which kept the population alive. That is as close to extinction as a population can fall. DNA analysis has further shown that in 1977 the Welsh population was enhanced by the immigration of a German female into the breeding stock, which helped to broaden the genetic base of the pairs in Wales and has quite clearly contributed in an important way to the modest consolidation of breeding success thereafter.

7 The Kite Worldwide

The kite is not only a bird of superlatives, it is also unique in several ways. One of these is that it is the only bird of prey which is almost entirely restricted to Europe. All our other European species of birds of prey are also to be found well outside the borders of Europe, either extending eastwards into Asia and the Middle East or southwards across the Mediterranean into Africa. Only the red kite can claim to be, to all intents and purposes, exclusively a European bird, with the only exceptions to this being occasional pairs from the vestigial populations which formerly bred in Morocco and Tunisia and may possibly still do so.

The red kite's present sparse distribution is only a shadow of what it was 100 years or more ago. The fragmented nature of its current range throughout the countries in which it still occurs, added to the catalogue of those from which it has been wholly lost, is evidence of the human persecution it has suffered over the years.

In northern and western Europe it was lost from Norway and Denmark by the end of the 19th century – although it has recently re-colonised south-east Jutland. In Holland it occurs only rarely and it probably no longer breeds in the Baltic States. Farther east and south, the breeding populations in western Russia, Hungary, southern Poland and northern parts of the Balkan states have disappeared. Thus, as can be seen from the map, kites are now reduced to parts of

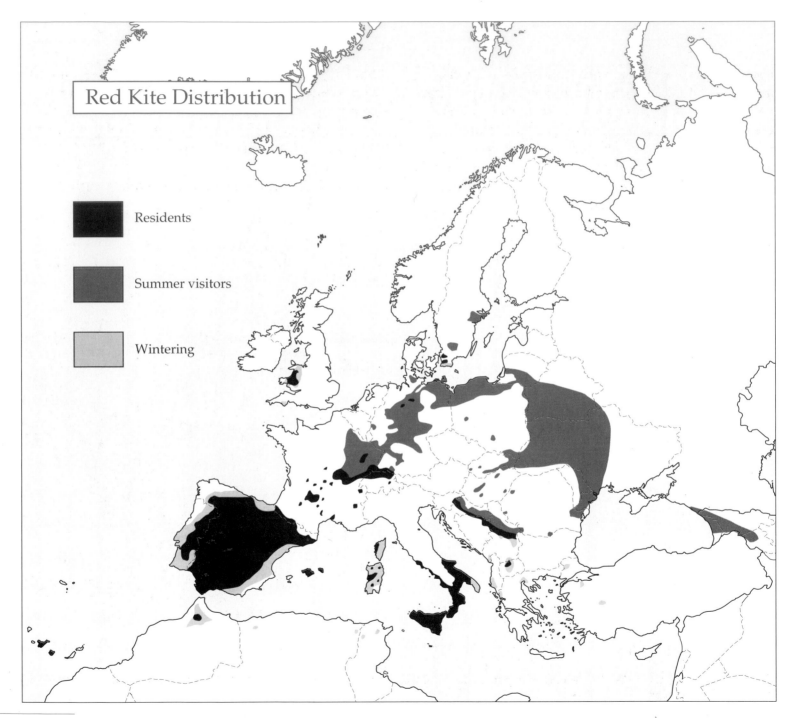

Red Kite Distribution

Residents

Summer visitors

Wintering

~ THE RED KITE ~

western Europe. Here, however, numbers are in fact increasing and the long-term prospects for its future in these areas are encouraging. The large populations in Germany and France are growing steadily and in Spain, despite persecution, numbers are being maintained. Countries such as Austria, Belgium and Denmark have been tentatively re-colonised in recent years. In other countries such as Czechoslovakia, Poland, Sweden and Wales, where populations are still very small, the red kite has gradually increased in recent years under careful protection. In Sweden the increase has been quite dramatic in a short time, from 50 pairs in 1980 to about 200 pairs in 1989.

The total world population of the red kite is now somewhere around 13,000 pairs.

. . . .

Map adapted from: Cramp *et al.: Handbook of the Birds of Europe, the Middle East and North Africa Vol. II* published Oxford University Press, 1980.

8 The Future

The red kite has suffered a tortured history over the past 400 years of its existence in Britain. Its demise tragically echoes that of several other bird of prey species which have succumbed at the hand of man over recent centuries. White–tailed sea eagle, osprey and goshawk were completely eliminated (but have since been re-established). Others such as golden eagle, hen harrier, and red kite were pushed back to tiny fringe populations in far corners of these islands. What then is the future for the red kite now that it has passed through the seemingly endless tunnel of uncertainty and has a base in Wales of over 100 pairs?

Threats to the Welsh breeding population still exist. Egg collectors, shamefully, are an annual problem and accidental disturbance to nesting pairs by walkers, picnickers or farming operations has accounted for the desertion or depredation of too many nests in the past. The most serious threat to the breeding population, however, is the illegal use of poisoned meat baits put down in the open to control foxes and crows. Although not intended for kites, the birds are among the first to find such baits and are very vulnerable to them. Analyses of many corpses over the years indicate that up to 60% of Welsh kites die prematurely as the result of feeding on such baits.

Previous page: Kites gathering above roost trees on a winter afternoon.

Despite these threats and problems, the future for the red kite can be viewed with some optimism. There are now probably more than 300 individual birds in Wales and their numbers are increasing gradually but encouragingly each year. When the weather in the nesting season is poor – as it so often is in Wales – the number of young reared is disappointing; in better springs (as in 1992 when 93 young were produced) the population will enjoy a clear upward surge which may be represented by an equivalent increase in breeding pairs a year or two later. In parallel to the gradual increase in numbers, the kites are beginning to edge outwards from their core area in Central Wales and extend their range a little more widely in Wales. As they do so they move onto more productive land and breeding success is improved.

Another major factor has come into play since 1989 which will have a huge impact on the future of the species. This was the decision by the (then) Nature Conservancy Council and RSPB to proceed with a five–year experimental programme of re-introduction of red kites into one area in England and another in northern Scotland. In the first year 10 young birds were brought into Scotland from Sweden and four were transported on to England where they were joined by a single chick from Wales. The process of re–introduction had begun and since then the progress of the introduced birds (all the later English ones came from Spain) has been quite startling and beyond anyone's best dreams.

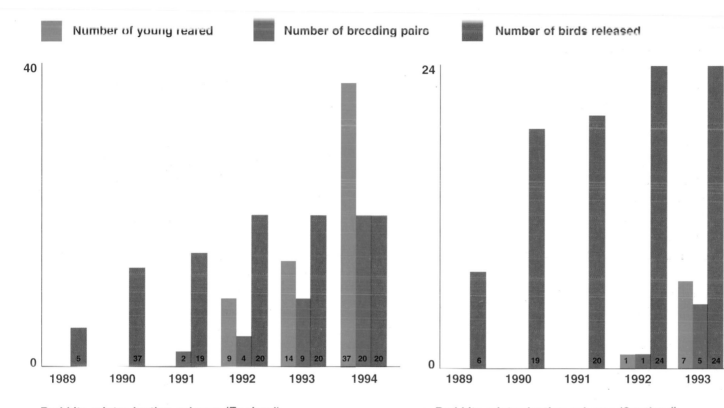

Red kite reintroduction scheme (England)

Red kite reintroduction scheme (Scotland)

There is no question that much of the countryside of Britain is still perfectly capable of supporting a viable population of this spectacular bird of prey, as the pilot re-introduction programmes have shown. With this in mind, and with the possibility of extended programmes of re-introduction into other areas, there is the real prospect that red kites could again fly over the fields and woodlands throughout the land in the not-too-distant future. This is its ancestral home – the whole of Britain – a range from which it has been dispossessed by man, a range in which, with the help of man, it could now be re-established.

The red kite is indeed no longer a bird of the past, but very much a bird of the future.

Female red kite at nest with five-week-old young.

Above: Wingtagging kites as part of the conservation programme has produced much important data about dispersal, pair formation and fidelity, seasonal movements and site loyalty.

Right: Kite eggs have been a serious target for egg collectors for over 100 years.

Far right: Poisoning, through baits put out illegally for foxes and crows, is the most serious threat to kites in Wales.

~ THE RED KITE ~

Previous page: The upper Tywi Valley. Classic kite country with small valley fields, scattered oak woodland, wide swathes of fridd land on the valley sides and open sheep walk above.

Below: Young rabbits are an important food item in Wales.

Right: The legendary Dinas Hill on the RSPB reserve in the upper Tywi valley – former traditional home of the last of the red kites – and Welsh folk hero Twm Sion Catti.

Left: The red kite's unique silhouette and striking colours make it unmistakable on the wing.

Above: In Wales, red kites always line their nests with sheep wool but frequently collect scraps of cloth or other rubbish for decoration.

~ THE RED KITE ~

~ THE RED KITE ~

Previous page: Sheep carrion is one of the most important food sources throughout the year in Wales.

Right: In late winter and early spring, kites will circle high above the nesting valleys on bright, clear days.

Far right: Nests are often in the main fork of a large oak.

~ THE RED KITE ~

Left: Circling over a nesting valley in late winter.

Above: Kite country is also sheep country. Sheep provide much food for the kites throughout the year – carrion and placentae.

Three chicks is a large clutch for kites in Wales. When food is scarce, fratricide is fairly common or the youngest siblings soon perish.

9 Kite Facts

Names
Red kite (*Milvus milvus*)

Welsh name
Barcud coch

Similar species
Black kite (*Milvus migrans*)
Migrant species; vagrant to Britain

Distribution
Virtually exclusive to Europe; formerly North Africa and Cape Verde Is.

Population
about 13,000 pairs mainly Central and SW Europe.

British populations
Formerly widespread and very numerous. Exterminated Scotland and England in 1870s. Welsh population (1994) 107 pairs plus about 100 additional individuals.

Status
Resident. Adult birds sedentary. Some juveniles disperse and return later.

Legal status
Annex 1 of EU Birds Directive.
Schedule 1 of Wildlife and Countryside Act 1981.
UK Red Data List of Birds (Species of UK Conservation Concern).

Habitats
Open country, with woodland, up to about 400 m. In Wales mainly restricted to remoter hilly areas with hanging valley oakwoods.

Measurements
Length (cm) 60-66
Wingspan (cm) 175-195
Weight (gm) 800-1600
(Females up to 5% larger than males.)

Nesting
March-August. Untidy nests built of sticks, lined with sheep's wool in trees in deciduous or mixed woods. Nests often decorated with paper, string and other rubbish.

Eggs and incubation
Normal clutch 2-3, occasionally 1 (usually because females are young) or 4. Eggs laid at 2-3 day intervals.
Incubation 31-32 days, mainly by female.

Fledging
8-10 week period. Young brooded by female for first 2-3 weeks.

Predators
Carrion crow, raven.

Food
Much carrion; scavenges rubbish tips etc and feeds extensively on carcases of sheep and other dead remains. Also true predator taking range of small mammals (up to small rabbits), invertebrates (notably earthworms), nestling birds; occasionally fish. Piratises freely from corvids etc.

Recommended reading *The Kite's Tale: the story of the Red Kite in Wales* by Roger Lovegrove, published by RSPB 1991.

The Royal Society for the Protection of Birds

The Royal Society for the Protection of Birds is *the* charity that takes action for wild birds and the environment. It has joined with the bird and habitat conservation organisations worldwide to form a global partnership called BirdLife International.

It was the RSPB who first developed the idea of the Kite Country green tourism project to enable people to come to Mid Wales to see the red kite and other species in their natural surroundings without posing any risk of disturbance to them.

Protecting wild birds is vitally important. One of the biggest threats they face is the loss of their habitats. When a woodland is cut down or a moorland is ploughed up, birds and other wildlife lose out – and we do too because part of our natural heritage is lost, possibly forever.

The RSPB strives to prevent these losses. It buys land that is under threat and manages and improves it so that it becomes a haven for all the wildlife it supports. The RSPB fights the threats of damaging development as well as neglect. But it needs your support – please join the RSPB today!

More information from RSPB Wales Office, Bryn Aderyn, The Bank, Newtown, Powys, SY16 2AB Tel: 01686 626678